WHAT'S A NICE GUY (OR GAL) LIKE YOU, DOING WITH A BOOK LIKE THIS?

You're doing what comes naturally.

It's only natural to want to talk and even more (and more and more) with that inviting someone sitting so close beside you and yet so far away.

It's only natural to want to find out how the best in the business perform the exquisite art of the pick-up.

It's only natural to have to hold on tight to keep from falling off your bar stool when you find out how far out people will go and how wildly they will reach for the line with the bait and the hook to make their catch and their night.*

*"I'd like to ask you out, but in ten years I plan to become a Supreme Court Justice."

*"Weren't you at my winning lottery ticket party?"

*"Is it hot in here or is it you?"

*Or any of the other head-turning, rib-tickling selections in—

1,001 GREAT PICK-UP LINES

Compiled by the Tanqueray-Sterling Vodka Bartender Survey, with all profits to the company going to T.J. Martell Foundation to combat leukemia.

1,001
GREAT PICK-UP LINES
Compiled from the

Tanqueray Sterling VODKA®

Annual Survey

Original Commentary and Editing by
Beverly Berwald

Illustrations by
Tracy Stephen Burroughs

A SIGNET BOOK

SIGNET
Published by the Penguin Group
Penguin Books USA Inc., 375 Hudson Street,
New York, New York 10014, U.S.A.
Penguin Books Ltd, 27 Wrights Lane,
London W8 5TZ, England
Penguin Books Australia Ltd, Ringwood,
Victoria, Australia
Penguin Books Canada Ltd, 10 Alcorn Avenue,
Toronto, Ontario, Canada M4V 3B2
Penguin Books (N.Z.) Ltd, 182–190 Wairau Road,
Auckland 10, New Zealand

Penguin Books Ltd, Registered Offices:
Harmondsworth, Middlesex, England

First published by Signet, an imprint of Dutton Signet,
a division of Penguin Books USA Inc.

First Printing, October, 1993
10 9 8 7 6 5 4 3 2 1

Contents

Introduction

If you want to find out how to successfully pick up men or women,

—you could spend days in a library combing through research papers on the human psyche, or

—load up on all the current how-to self-help books at your local bookstore, or

—cut through the tedium, save both money and time, and read this book. It's full of the best pick-up lines from bartenders, Tanqueray drinkers, and other people from all over the country. We roamed up and down the East and West Coasts and all through the states in between to get their story on the mating ritual between the sexes. We thought it was about time someone listened to the bartenders, those uncredentialed experts. They've spent countless hours observing the Art of the Pick-up. Their meticulous cataloguing of human nature has served them well in dealing with the public. They can tell you blindfolded who's who just by the line that either rolls or stumbles off a person's tongue. They *know* dialogue, their antennae are keen to the differences between a banker, a construction worker, a jock, an office worker, a stockbroker—the list goes on ad infinitum. Because they've fine-honed their people watching/listening, in some instances, they can silently mouth the line even before it's said. If a picture says a thousand words, one pick-up line speaks a thousand pictures about the person saying it, according to the bartenders we interviewed. But in some cases, the nation's bartenders admitted there was no telling what might come out of a person's mouth. That's why we also polled bar-goers and just plain folks, all of whom were gifted with outrageous imaginations. All the faithful who continue to take their seats alongside the bar have their own charm. Each has their own choice lines, their own brand of humor. However similar or dissimilar to the person next to them, they join the perpetual and exciting dance between the sexes. (One bartender aptly called it "live theater.")

A case in point: we've all had that feeling that Fate was intervening on more than one occasion. You only just left a relationship, and who should be sitting on the stool next to you? You can't BELIEVE IT! The person is just too gorgeous for words. You've got to seize the moment! You flip through the file cabinet in your brain . . . Do you comment on the obvious; their sky blue eyes, their adorable nose, or their fabulous cheekbones? Or do you turn the topic to neutral territory like yesterday's Cubs game or the weekend weather? Perhaps neither, or maybe both of the above. But whatever you do, you must *tickle them with your wit* so they find you absolutely irresistible. Live dangerously, wing it, invent on the spur of the moment. Or if you prefer (keep in mind, you want to stimulate laughter and interest) consult the experts in *1001 Great Pick-up Lines*—quick!—before they get away.

Now the question is, do you open with a pun or an innuendo? And just how do you want to serve it? Wrapped around the topic of food, sex, or real estate? Or maybe you lean toward the philosophical. Or the political. Whatever strikes your fancy, read on. The table of contents has a veritable banquet of topics to choose from. Just remember, it's all in the delivery. So be confident and have fun! If you like yourself, so will that person next to you. That seems to be the consensus among the experts on both sides of the bar.

Accountants

Not so conservative as you think, these bottom line folks. When they've left their ledgers and calculators behind for the day, watch out! She may not take off her Brooks Brothers jacket, and he may not even loosen his tie, but their spirits are yearning to break loose and have a party. And if they had their druthers, they'd just as soon have an indoor barbecue in the lounge. But mind you, their fun is all very orderly. No rock star antics here (our apologies to all the rock stars who never turned a room upside down). Kind and considerate, Mr. and Ms. Accountant will go out of their way to accommodate. (Maybe they're stung by a twinge of guilt when they have to break the tax news.) But not to worry, they're not about to roll over and play doormat either. Underneath all that decorum is a very healthy streak of cynicism. Terrific at sizing up the situation, they'll probably approach with a straightforward offer to join them for a drink. After all, the shortest possible distance between two people *is* the truth. But once accountants have made their intentions obvious, they'll give themselves permission to fly. Witness, among the following lines, not a negative to be found—they're a positive bunch.

I'm sorry for staring, but you look like someone I used to know.

•

Shall we talk or continue flirting from a distance?

•

May I have the honor and privilege of sitting next to you?

•

I won a great prize for my pick-up line. Would you like to hear it? "Hi!"

•

Excuse me, I think it's time we met.

•

Actually, I tend to make normal conversation rather than try to dazzle someone with a Kamikaze one-liner.

•

You're the one I've been saving this seat for.

•

Were we supposed to meet for dinner?

•

What did you say? Oh, I thought you were talking to me?

•

Gosh, you're pretty.

•

You're very easy on the eyes.

•

Your smile is like sunshine.

•

God must have been in a very good mood the day we met.

•

You are the reason men fall in love.

•

Do you have room in your life for a new friend?

•

I just moved into the building and I was wondering if you could recommend a good restaurant in the neighborhood. Would you like to join me?

•

You know, I'm not just an interesting person, I have a body, too.

•

There is more than what meets the eyes.

•

I'm sensing the intense feeling you have for me . . . is it my cologne?

•

I would say I like you, but you'd think I'm trying to pull a fast one.

•

What can I do to make you mine?

•

Would you care for a drink? I'll buy you a Tanqueray!

•

I had a dream about you last night. Would you like to make it a reality?

•

You should be someone's wife.

•

If he doesn't show, I'll be right over here.

•

So there you are! I've been looking all over for you.

•

I've been trying to meet a person like you for hours now.

•

Hey, I need your help! My mother says if I don't get a date this weekend, she's putting me up for adoption.

•

I'm fighting the urge to make you the happiest woman on earth tonight.

•

Are you free tonight or will it cost me?

•

Let's talk about "early retirement."

Ad Men and Women

They work hard to keep their clients happy, some of which are the U.S.'s major corporations. When you've got only 30 to 60 seconds to sell a product, every millisecond of genius counts and costs. And if sales don't shoot up overnight, who's to blame? The ad agency. They lose the account—how about a couple of million for starters?—and the creative people, the ones with the ideas, are out of a job. Fair enough? No. But who said life is fair? Somebody's got to be the fall guy or gal. It could be the product that's responsible for lean sales and have nothing to do with the product's advertising. But when corporations open Fort Knox to pay the ad bill, they expect the magicians of advertising to pull tricks out of a hat. Pressure, anybody? No, never. Only a tightrope act comes near to being so risky.

Next time you're sitting near some of the creative people from an ad agency, cock an ear in their direction—their creativity isn't confined to their offices. They're long on marathons of fast wit volleyed back and forth over the martinis. Nothing escapes their attention—everything's fodder for their absurd commentary.

Excuse me but I'm doing my thesis on stamina. Would you be interested in finding the true meaning of marathon?

•

Of all my relationships, I like sexual the best.

•

Darling, you haven't changed a bit since our divorce.

•

[Without waiting for them to say anything] Fine! And you?

•

This is your lucky day, because I just happen to be single.

•

You're the most beautiful woman I've ever met . . . today.

•

You know you might be asked to leave, you make the other men look bad.

•

Just where do those legs end?

•

What lovely eyes you have, are they yours or did you buy them?

•

You know, my mother says you have the best posture of anyone I know.

•

The best of me is behind me.

•

The guy I'm with, oh, he's my brother.

•

Would you like someone to mix with your drink?

•

Would you like to come back to my place and pet my dog?

•

Did I used to dunk your pigtails in the inkwell in grammar school?

•

Can I be your slave for tonight?

•

Be different, say yes.

•

We voted you "The most beautiful girl here" and the grand prize is me.

I'm in advertising. Would you like to be in our next photo shoot?

•

We voted you "The Most Beautiful Girl Here" and the grand prize is me.

•

Picture this, you, me, bubble baths, and hot fudge sundaes.

•

Do you believe in the hereafter. Well, then I guess you know what I'm here after.

•

Motel spelled backward is letom.

•

So, do you like bagels or muffins in the morning?

•

When's our wedding?

•

Bring on the gin, we've just found the tonic.

•

Can I end this sentence with a proposition?

•

Excuse me, weren't you Shirley MacLaine in a past life?

•

Weren't we married in a past life?

•

My parents met at a place like this. Let's get the hell out of here.

•

Funny, you don't look like a Republican.

Actors and Actresses

There's a rumor that you never have to worry about actors or actresses saying anything bad about you because they're too busy talking about themselves. To a certain extent that's true. But don't forget all good salesmen get jazzed when they talk about their product. And for those in the acting profession, they *are* the product. So next time the guy or gal next to you at the bar excitedly launches into a short dissertation on the last audition they performed gloriously well at, give them a chance. Come on, folks, it's a living and a hard one at that. Ninety-five percent of the actors are unemployed or working second and third jobs; the other five percent are millionaires many times over. Can you blame actors if they get carried away when the possibility of working looms brightly on their horizon? Besides, once they get the chance to spill over with enthusiasm to someone who's genuinely listening, watch how quickly they'll turn the conversation to you. Twas a wise person who once said that as soon as a hungry soul is satisfied, he can think about feeding the soul next to him. Actors and actresses are a tough-spirited breed apart from the rest of the human species. And because they're used to playing a variety of roles, there's an easy give and take between them and most people. They don't get sucked into people's moods. None of us should. We're all playing roles, only the actor is profoundly aware of it. That's why he doesn't take himself or others quite so seriously. You'll see from the following choice pickup lines:

Hi, I'm employed.

•

Mind if I stare at you close up
instead of from across the room?

•

Perhaps you recognize me from
adult movies.

•

There's an aura about you that's hidden, and I want to bring that aura out.

•

Which is easier? Getting into those pants, or getting out of them?

•

What's your sign?

•

[To a female] I want to bear all your children.

•

Love is like a rug . . . walk all over me . . . lie on me . . . but no animals allowed.

•

Your eyes, they're as blue as window cleaner.

•

Are those your real eyes?

•

Excuse me, but did you happen to find my Congressional Medal of Honor?

•

Whatever you do, don't ever cut your hair!

•

Weren't you a woman the last time we met?

•

Would you like to take a shower?

•

I'm very comfortable talking with you now that I'm back in men's clothing full-time.

•

You bring new meaning to the word "alien."

•

Take a chance.

•

Always good for you to see me again.

•

Are you actually beautiful or do you remind me of myself?

•

If life is a meat market, you're prime rib.

•

Would you like to be in movies?

•

Don't you know me from somewhere?

•

I'm filthy rich and have 6 weeks to live.

•

My rank is a naval inspector. Let's go to your place for an inspection.

•

Here's your chance to get to know me.

•

I'm choking, I need mouth to mouth.

•

I'm trying to determine after years of therapy and lots of testing, whether or not I'm allergic to sex.

•

I've been noticing you not noticing me.

•

I'm lost. Which way to your house?

•

Excuse me for not getting up. I broke my ankle falling off my polo pony.

Bakers

They rise so early they jump into clothes still warm from the night before. But let us dispel any mistaken illusions—you won't find them sleepwalking through their days. They can't afford to. They deal with machines and equipment so powerful they could end up as smooth as cake batter if they were anything but alert.

As one bartender said, talking to a baker is like listening to part chemist, part artist, part comic. They have to be precise, be skilled at weights and measures—a little off can mean the loss of a bunch of money and an entire reputation.

Why is it the same recipe can be followed by several bakers, but the end results are vastly different? That's where the art comes in—a certain intuition and a tender affection for food can render a croissant an oral and visual masterpiece.

The comic streak in a baker leaps out when he has to chase down accounts receivable—hey, how do you repossess last month's shipment of danish that has long since been happily consumed by a hotel or restaurant's patrons. Your only recourse is to hold next month's brioche hostage.

They take everything all in good stride— nothing can get this tremendous bundle of energy and intellect down. As most are either European imports—German, Austrian, and French—or Americans trained in the European tradition, they seem to take in the greater picture of life, which liberates them from the petty. Life's too short to be serious as you'll witness from their pick-up lines below.

Are you interested in a hot slice of conversation?

•

There must be something wrong with my eyes, I can't take them off you.

•

You smell delicious!

•

I thought women like you traveled in packs.

•

My drink is getting lonely, would you like to join me?

•

So when do you think we'll go metric?

•

I'm just a caraway seed in the bakery of life.

•

Sweetness is my weakness.

•

You're so sweet, you're gonna put sugar out of business.

•

The better the batter, the better the butter.

•

Hi, are those really yours?

•

I have season tickets to the Bulls' games.

•

I was, am, and will be crazy about you.

•

I can raise your blood pressure.

•

I'd gladly give up celibacy to be with you.

•

I'm an organ donor, need anything?

•

I'm fit to be tied . . . and caressed and kissed and . . .

•

Let's go lie down and talk about it.

•

Nothing tastes as good as you look.

•

You must be lost, because I have never seen anyone so beautiful in this place before.

•

I know my mother would just love you.

•

Say, didn't we meet at Woodstock?

•

Today has been a dark cloud. Would you care to be a silver lining?

•

What time do you have to be back in heaven?

•

You are truly beautiful. Can you cook?

•

I'm looking for something unusual. What do you recommend?

•

You're what God imagined when He said, "Let there be woman."

•

You make my eyeballs happy.

•

Did you just smile, or was that the sun coming out?

•

You look like an angel. Welcome to Earth.

•

I seem to have lost my phone number. Can I have yours?

•

This menu looks good, but you're the most delicious thing here.

Bankers

Decked out in regulation gray flannel, you may think the banker's sewn up tight. Check again. Underneath the conservative front is a giggler. Underneath the giggler is a person who loves all things sensual, who wields a glib tongue as easily as some show biz comedians. The only difference—he or she stars in the local lounge, with no lights, no cameras, no media attention. Just the folks within earshot are privy to a banker's wit.

So, if you're in the market for quick repartee and electrifying sensual wit, bankers score among the highest. It has something to do with their timing and the greatest aphrodisiac in the world—money. They hang around it all day. They rub up against it. They smell it, touch it, dream it, live it—they're marinated in it. It lubes the synapses, gets the neurons working at optimum speed. All their senses heightened by this little green magic, the banker's brain can't help but go wild when they cut loose from their citadels of power. It's called the giddy factor. It's the flip side of the serious factor. The equation goes something like this. The greater the occupational risk—what could be riskier than gambling a bank's resources on million-dollar loans?—the greater the need for pure, unharnessed joy!

Hi, I'm interested, what's your name?

•

You must be the real reason for global warming.

•

My sign's right-away, what's yours?

•

If we're not related, I'd like to be.

•

So what are the chances that we can engage in anything more than just conversation?

•

My God, Charles Darwin was right!

•

I saw your picture today . . . in the dictionary next to the word beautiful.

•

I never knew dollies came full grown.

•

If I tell you that you have a nice body, would you hold it against me?

•

Do fries come with that shake?

•

You know what would look great on you? Me!

•

That dress would look great on my bedroom floor.

•

Wasn't I married to you once?

•

We've gotta go on meeting like this.

•

What time do you get off and how?

•

Is it a coincidence that your blouse matches my bedspread?

•

What are we doing later—tomorrow and the next day?

•

Are you busy the rest of this month?

•

I've been desperately seeking someone of your caliber to explain the universe to me.

•

What do you say we give our genes a chance to become congenial?

•

Wouldn't we look cute on a wedding cake together?

•

Will you marry me for an hour?

•

If I could be anything, I'd love to be your bathwater.

•

Would you rather go out or stay in for breakfast in the morning?

•

Do you like chunky or smooth peanut butter?

•

We cannot direct the wind, but we certainly can adjust the sails.

•

Help the homeless. Take me home.

•

I promise I'll respect you in the morning.

Chefs

Ever look at a Picasso from his ultra-abstract period or an Escher painting with stairs climbing out of walls? That's how most chefs feel after spending a third of their day behind a sizzling stove. Imagine cooking for hundreds of people in one afternoon. You've got to be able to handle dozens of things at once. Part juggler, part orchestra conductor, timing is everything to a chef. On top of those variables, you've got to deal with the fastidious patrons who want their pasta *between* al dente and soft. Huh? If the food's not just so, those same patrons will storm into the kitchen and chastise the cook.

It's a wonder chefs are not all raving maniacs by the end of their shifts. Fortunately, most chefs observe the creed, "grace under pressure." But once they've fulfilled their culinary duties and flee the kitchen, anything goes. Remember, they're hot; their gray matter's been swelling and so have their libidos. They could just as easily light out and do a last tango, or wrestle you on the lounge carpet as drink a Tanqueray-Sterling Collins. They'll probably do all three. No telling what's going to issue from their mouths, but guaranteed, it will probably shock you, or at least make you laugh.

•

Hello, I'm new to this country and you are the prettiest sight I've seen. Can you give me a tour of your body?

•

My name is ———. Remember it because you'll be screaming it later tonight.

•

Is it hot in here or is it just you?

•

You remind me of bacon, the way you sizzle.

•

Is this love on a two-way street?

•

Hi! I like tacos, '63 cabernets, and my favorite color is magenta. How 'bout you?

•

You make me melt like hot fudge on a sundae.

•

Can I taste your drink? [Then lean over and kiss him or her.]

•

Are we in the frozen food section, or are you just happy to see me?

•

That wine brings out the bloodshot in your eyes.

•

Pardon me, but don't you recognize me with clothes on?

•

I love to cook. Do you like to eat?

•

What do you cook your catfish in? Peanut or safflower oil?

•

You want a lobster dinner?

•

Excuse me, could you tell me how long it takes to cook a leg of lamb?

•

So you're a vegetarian, too!

•

Come into the garden and see my tomatoes.

•

How would you like for me to cook you breakfast?

•

So what do you do besides make me warm all over?

•

I'm not asking you to marry me, I'm just asking you for a dance.

•

You have the sexiest behind. . . . I just couldn't resist taking a closer look.

•

You look so different with your clothes on.

•

Let's have a party and invite your pants down.

•

You know I've always wanted to sleep with you.

•

I wonder what our children will look like.

•

Can I light your fire—I mean cigarette?

•

I am not drunk, I am intoxicated by you.

•

One way or the other, I'm going to have you tonight. You might as well be there.

•

I'd like to know the ingredients in the recipe that cooked you up.

Classical Musicians

Shyer than shy, these gentle souls impress with a sense of what's proper and upright. Some may call them conservative. Others, old-fashioned. Whatever. Driven by the sublime, their lives are devoted to the appreciation of Bach, Mozart, Beethoven, or latter-day masters. Rigorously loyal to their art, they spend hours each day practicing their instruments, refining their ears, and interpreting the great composers' original intents. The discipline required is a grueling test of endurance. But these are no mere mortals. The simple fact is, classical musicians are descendents of the gods. But check the flipside of any self-respecting Apollo and you'll find a Bacchus chomping at the bit for a little revelry. As titans of genius, musicians have a capacity for intellect matched only by their appetites for merriment. Just examine how well they live up to their renown for dizzying pleasure. If their pick-up lines are any indication, they get the highest marks for innuendo. All things sensual, tantalizing, and titillating are the domain of these bacchanalians.

My heart is beating like a drum, you are so beautiful.

•

Is that your smile or did you pay for it?

•

No, that's not a banana.

•

I know there are thousands of perfect guys out there, but only four of us don't watch football.

•

Go ahead, make a pass at me.

•

Your place or your place.

•

I bet I can tell you what's on my mind.

•

So you are the reason my insides are doing a dance.

•

That's enough of undressing me with your eyes, let's get out of here.

•

There's a fire in my apartment. Would you like to go get warm?

•

I'm available for the next hour.

•

Come with me to the Casbah, we could make beautiful music together.

•

So, what time do we get off?

•

Let's exchange some Family Values.

•

I'll make you see God.

•

Do you sleep on your stomach?
No! Can I?

•

Is your wife married? I hope not
cause I'd like to be your fiancée.

•

Let's go into the stairwell so I can
... um ... sing you a song. The
acoustics are terrible in here.

•

If beauty were music you'd be a
symphony.

•

Is it just me, or does everyone here have a pick-up line?

•

So what part of Heaven are you from?

•

Your voice is music to my ears.

•

Why don't I go up to your place and see you sometime?

•

We can make beautiful music together.

•

I saw you play in the band, I'm quite adept with a G string myself!

•

You can pluck my strings anytime (at a musician's convention).

•

You're hot stuff!

•

If I could be anything, I'd be your body lotion.

•

[Looking at shirt tag] I was checking to see if it said, "Made in Heaven."

•

There are two things I'd like to say to you, "Good night" and "Good Morning."

•

Where were you the first time you heard this song?

Computer Programmers

They could wrap circles around you with their energy. But they have nothing to prove to anyone, because they quietly prove it everyday to themselves: they're the gods of electronics. It comes from dialoguing with Mac-Brains all day long. There's nothing more empowering than pressing buttons and getting results lightning fast. You'd think with all their wizardry, they'd develop bloated egos. Quite the opposite: balanced is what readily comes to mind, then downright earthy, innocent, and good-natured. Those are just a few of the ways you'd best describe them. Add to that playful, yes, but terribly proper. So you might just find them smiling at you shyly, although on other occasions, we've caught them being quite candid.

Was that you? Oh, I thought so!

•

Were you checking me out, or did my ego kick in?

•

What format is your PC?

•

So how will I see you again?

•

The force has sent me here to save you. Take my hand and come quickly.

•

When you need a hug or just someone to talk to, I'll be there.

•

If I told you that you have a great smile you'd probably think I was trying to pick you up. You have a great smile and I am.

•

I'm a math major. What's your cosine?

•

Hypothetically, what lines are effective with a person like you?

•

I'm not picking you up, I picked you out.

•

Would you like to come see my computer-generated etchings?

•

Looking at you makes my beeper start to vibrate.

•

You are why I came in here alone.

•

I felt a flow of positive kinetic energy hit me when you entered the room.

•

Did anyone ever tell you that you have the most pulchritudinous orbs?

•

Excuse me, do you think we might have a mutual friend who could introduce us?

•

How do you feel about adopting boyfriends if you can't have one on your own?

•

Let's sit together and rejoice.

•

My friends are leaving but I'd love it if you gave me a reason to stay.

•

I want you. Let's get out of here!

•

If I drink one of these, I may forget how to get back to the monastery.

•

Is it me or are we the only two not trying to score?

•

No wonder the sky is gray today, all the blue is in your eyes.

•

Where did you get your freckles from?

•

You've got the smile I'd like to wake up to.

•

You make me so nervous, I've completely forgotten my standard pick-up line.

•

Your laptop or mine.

•

What's so funny, are you falling in love?

•

Can we look into the future together?

•

It's a jungle out there, so let me be your guide.

•

You I love and not another.

Construction Workers

There aren't any safety nets down below, but they catwalk around skyscrapers as though it's only a foot-long drop. They ride steel girders that seesaw thirty stories above a traffic maze. They scale the sides of buildings with as much certainty as skilled mountain climbers. Fearlessly they rise above the rest of us each day to obtain a perspective on life that reminds them just how small all of us really are. They might as well be astronauts gazing down at earthlings from outer space, for they learn what most of us forget: everything and nothing is important all at once. If that's the case, then we haven't got time to waste. A soul-humbling lesson, yes, but one that wakes you up, makes you free. Tells you the only real value in life is to love and be happy. The rest is pretense, lacking in any substance. Must be the reason why construction workers know how to cut to the chase. Read their smiles and their pick-up lines: seize the moment—that's all we have!

Hi, those jeans seem to be working overtime. What time are they getting off?

•

I'd gladly give you the shirt off my back, if you'd take the rest of me with it.

•

Excuse me for staring, but I love the view.

•

I'll bet you cause a lot of construction-zone riots.

•

Is there a fire in here or are we just standing too close?

•

I know you, I dreamt about you last night.

•

Did I see you in a magazine?

•

Didn't I see you in the latest beauty pageant?

•

You look like someone I'd like to talk to.

•

Let me be your coffee mug in the morning, your candy bar at noon, and your cool creamy dessert in the evening.

•

What would it take for a guy like me to go out with a girl like you?

•

I'm not like all the rest of the guys, honest.

If we were alone together, what would you do to entertain us?

Can I wrap you up and bring you home?

Would you like to watch the sunrise together?

I bet there's a whole lot of woman under that dress.

Our chromosones were meant to be together.

You look like you need a real man.

You could use some more protein in your diet.

•

Do you indulge in sports?

•

How could I ask a woman of such striking beauty to give up the Roller Derby?

•

I have no fleas, I'm faithful, and I promise to wear my collar and dog tags at all times.

•

What is the difference between a brick and a blonde? When you lay a brick it doesn't follow you around for a week.

•

The split between your teeth is the sexiest thing I've ever seen.

•

You're so hot you give me the chills.

I have no fleas, I'm faithful, and I promise to wear my collar and dog tags at all times.

•

Your mind is what interests me the most.

•

I never pass up an opportunity to say hello to a beautiful woman.

•

Since you're an angel this must be heaven.

•

The last time I saw you I was dreaming.

•

You don't have to play Lotto to get lucky.

•

If you got those eyes from your mother, I know why your dad married her.

•

[When a woman has on all red] I see you have your devil's suit on tonight.

•

You're hotter than Georgia asphalt on a summer day.

•

Your daddy must have been a bricklayer, because you sure have a great foundation.

•

Are you the most beautiful creature here or is that just my opinion?

•

You remind me of a meter maid I once knew.

•

Damn, baby, if beauty were a crime, you'd be doin' life.

Dental Hygienists

Thank God for these people, or else we'd all be toothless wonders. Next time you smile, think of your hygienist fondly, and floss a little extra in his or her honor. That's the best way, and also the most effective way, we can show our appreciation for them. Of course, dentists deserve their place in the sun as well, but hygienists are the unsung heroes—they're the first to alert us before it's too late. But it's much more than their prevention that deserves our praise here. They have a high tolerance level for monotony. Day in and day out, they cart away the plaque, leaving our teeth polished and feeling brand new. One would think that sooner or later they'd tire of this whole business of mouths.

But hygienists are a perservering lot, possessed of dignity and reserve. While the dignity carries over into their off-hours, the reserve doesn't (members of our survey). Hygienists have been known to surrender to laughing fits. It's when they pause for air, that the pick-up lines slip out of their mouths, just in time for their next round of laughter.

Excuse me, you have a sensuous overbite.

•

So you floss!

•

Hi, my friend wants to know your name.

•

Are you smiling at me or do I have my contacts in wrong?

•

You have the whitest teeth I've ever seen.

•

Trust me, I'm trained in oral hygiene.

•

I'm on smile patrol. You have exceeded the smile speed limit.

•

You look familiar. Aren't you that guy from my dreams?

•

Wow! Weren't you on some soap opera before?

•

You're one of the Chippendale dancers, aren't you?

•

May I have your autograph?

•

Can you come out and play tonight?

•

Is it possible that we may see one another again?

•

I've been waiting all my life for someone like you.

•

What's your blood type?

•

Feel free to buy me a drink anytime.

•

Hey, are you with the program or not?

•

Do you need a ride home?

•

Excuse me, can you give me directions to your heart?

•

Your opportunity for total fulfillment has arrived.

•

How about a hot date?

•

You don't know me, but you'd like to.

•

If you think that's funny, you should see me naked.

•

I think I was your blanket in a previous life.

•

I'd love to be a bar of soap in your shower.

•

You look so sweet you're giving me a toothache.

•

Wasn't it you who pinched me in the fifth grade?

•

What's your name, so I'll know who I'll be dreaming about tonight?

•

If you're not doing anything with your lips, how would you like to talk to me?

•

It's not the heat, it's not the humidity, it's you!

Developers

While most of us are tucked away at night dreaming of the simple pleasures in life, developers lie awake imagining the location of town houses, condos, skyscrapers. Their manifest destiny: I find, I tear down, I build up. It steels their nerves, propels their blood, gives meaning to their lives. With the new world conquered long ago, these modern-day explorers find purpose in rediscovering what's already there.

"The world's going through a lot of changes, and I can feel it right here at the bar," said one man we spoke to in Westlake, California. He got onto the subject of developers, since they make up quite a few of his regulars. "Different, just different," he went on. "They don't just go in and mow down trees and level hills anymore." Short-sightedness is being replaced by long-range thinking.

It's a heady feeling envisioning the possibilities of a resort community, for example: It's even headier to conceive of this same resort community blending into the environment! Work *with* nature instead of against it. Now that's a bold vision! And that's the newest crop of developers coming up today! You can spot them by their wonderful energy. You can feel that energy in their pick-up lines as well:

I suppose you've heard all the pick-up lines, haven't you?

•

Was that you or did the earth just move?

•

Excuse me, didn't we spend a week in the Bahamas together?

•

Are you the one?

•

Are you a local landmark?

•

Is the sun shining this brightly or could I possibly be blinded by your beauty?

•

So how many years in a row were you beauty queen?

•

Please talk to me a few minutes. It's good for me to be seen with a beautiful woman.

•

I would love to be the sod under your feet.

•

I'd buy you a drink but I'd be jealous of the glass.

•

If I were Adam and you were Eve, would you really make me wear a fig leaf?

•

Listen, I bought you some candy and flowers, but I left them at home. I thought maybe you and I could go back there and retrieve them.

•

I'd make you forget your last home!

•

I wish I were a bath towel so you could use me every day.

•

If I were your shower, I'd always be turned on.

•

Would you deny a dying man's last wish?

•

Will you marry me?

•

My husband doesn't understand me.

•

If I bought you a Tanqueray-Sterling Vodka, would you give me a kiss?

•

I've seen a lot of beautiful women, but you're a fantasy.

•

If I could build a woman from scratch, she'd look like you.

•

I'd like you with a twist of lime.

•

I'm hot as a firecracker and you look like a great match.

•

If you get any closer I'll need more ice!

•

Sure I'm with somebody. I'm with you.

•

I'm your type—"rich."

•

I saw you walk in. May I take you shopping?

•

I'm hot as a firecracker and you look like a great match.

I'm the best thing that's ever happened to you.

•

I'm psychic, last night I dreamt I woke up next to you.

•

Hi, I'm new in town, where can I get my Ferrari convertible serviced?

•

I'm looking for a good masseuse, do you know any?

•

Engineers

It used to be that all engineers were men. Not anymore. It's the '90's and women are joining their ranks in droves. Ever notice how engineers speak in a lingo that baffles the majority of us bipeds, with their references to calculus, velocity, tensile strength, etc.? They're a spatially oriented bunch, and in case you weren't aware, that means they can fasten on to a mechanical concept and follow it through from beginning to end. (Unlike a sizeable chunk of the population who turn apoplectic at the design of a can opener.) In other words, an engineer's grasp on life is pretty solid. In fact, a good many of the consumers we interviewed said they've gotten into some challenging debates with engineers. One interviewee said he never learned more about government and politics than from a woman who designed hard drives for a computer hardware company. Another man said he'd gotten a crash course in physics in one afternoon from a fellow patron who worked at an aerospace firm across the street. Rest assured, these spatially oriented folks are not big on small talk; there's not a lot of game playing. They'll let you know up front, and there's a touch of the romantic in them. All adds up to a breath of fresh air—you'll see, right below.

Hi, where were you all these beers?

•

Is this seat taken and are you?

•

Great things come in great packages.

•

Wow! You're breathtaking.

•

Excuse me, but I just had to come up to you and say hello.

•

Did it hurt? When you fell from heaven!

·

You are the best-looking guy/girl in this bar, and I can't keep my eyes off you.

·

Excuse me, can I have my heart back?

·

You've got a great pair of . . . shoulders.

·

You're so beautiful, are you a model?

·

Are you here for the magazine layout?

•

Weren't you Miss September?

•

So when does your centerfold come out?

•

Why did you quit making adult movies?

•

Aren't you the man of my dreams?

•

Am I bothering you? You sure bother me.

•

I would like you to be the mother of my children.

•

You look like you could use my company.

•

Would you like a drink?

•

Beauty is in the eye of the beholder, and I hope I'll be holding you tonight.

•

I wouldn't kick you out of bed for eating crackers.

•

If I were a transmission, you'd be my clutch.

•

I never thought I'd see a dream come to life.

•

I want to be the oxygen you breathe.

•

I could never say anything but yes to you.

•

My mother would love to see me with a girl like you.

•

I don't make much money, but I'm well endowed.

•

I'm not a religious man, but God sure does good work.

•

I would like to shake your world.

•

If you're as smart as you're good-looking, I think I'm in trouble.

Flight Attendants

Several thousand feet in the air, doing a balancing act amidst pockets of turbulence, and hungry passengers can get to you, if you let them. But flight attendants don't. They're tough inside, even though they're all smiles on the outside. Expected to play the gracious host or hostess, they must rise to the occasion forty hours a week. Just suppose one to two hundred people came for dinner and drinks, then fell asleep in *your* living room? Try that fantasy on for size or have a nightmare instead, whichever comes first. And yet these courteous specimens of good breeding never lose it, even when one of the problem "guests" gets a little irritable or demanding. Or when another can't resist telling the flight attendant the unabridged version of her life's story. Surely many wonderful solutions may race across the attendant's mind, such as a passenger eject button. But amazingly, flight attendants don't scheme to get even. They are the nicest among us. Even when they're not in uniform, you can recognize them in the lounge. They're the ones dishing out a little sardonic wit, mimicking the unforgettable moments in their travels, and volleying the best of the pick-up lines.

Are we near an airport or is that just the sound of my heart taking off?

•

Hi, I'm a free agent looking for a contract.

•

Lose the luggage. Come fly with me.

•

Is there a rich man in the house?

•

And what firm are you the CEO of?

•

What's a nice boy like you doing in a place like this?

•

I'm not sure what you saw in your mirror this morning, but I'm impressed.

•

Would you like a drink? Well, then get me one while you're at it.

•

You look very sensuous tonight.

•

Ask me where I've been all your life.

•

Is this fate or have you been following me?

•

So what's your favorite indoor sport?

•

Oh, why don't we just skip all the formalities and go right to marriage?

•

I'm looking for a strong man to flip my mattress.

•

I'm available if you are.

•

Mind if I borrow your friend? I promise to bring him back in the morning.

•

Weren't you in last month's GQ?

•

Did not we meet at the religious retreat last year?

•

I'm having a small party.

•

If you ever need love I'm just a phone call away.

•

I'm new in town. Can you give me the quickest directions to your house?

•

That's a great T-shirt. Can I talk you out of it?

•

What are we doing later on?

•

I'll be Ken, you be Barbie.

•

Is this seat taken as much as I am with you?

•

My mother wants me to marry you.

•

Is it hard to be easy, or easy to be hard?

•

Our children would be gorgeous.

•

Only you can tame my spirits with Tanqueray.

•

Smile if you had any.

•

It's been a very busy day, so why don't you lie back and I'll fill you in?

•

Weren't we great lovers in another life?

Jocks

Utterly charming in their lack of pretense, these Janes and Tarzans just flat out let you know what's on their minds. Come swing with me is the message. And when it's over, let's go pump some iron. Yo. No time to mince words. They're into the flesh—as in eight hours a day—toning, trimming, reconditioning for that next game, match, tournament. To a professional athlete, strategy is everything. Truth is simple. Success is timing. Some of that same simplicity is carried over into their off-hours. No need to clutter up their social life with convoluted moves, just get to the point.

Hi, if you're a runner, Can I be your shorts?

•

You seem very athletic.

•

Yeah, I used to play for the Chicago Bears.

•

Do you play any sports? How about tonsil hockey?

•

What size bowling ball do you use?

•

Anyone seen my Olympic Medals around here?

•

Hey, baby, you look like somebody I've seen before!

•

Are you here for the beauty contest?

•

Is Miss July your real name?

•

I've seen the rest, you're definitely the best.

•

Honey, you're so good-looking I'll stop watching football.

•

Want to be my mud-wrestling training partner? Let's practice in my tub.

•

You and me, perfect together.

•

You look great. . . . Do you work out?

•

Weren't you at the gym this morning?

•

What kind of physical exercise keeps you in such good shape?

•

Which health club do you work out at?

•

Wow, you are obviously an aerobics instructor—where do I sign up for your class?

•

Want to work out in my private gym?

•

So what's your target heart rate?

•

Kiss me hard enough and maybe I'll stop looking like a frog.

•

This place looks so much better when you're in it.

•

Are you looking for something in particular, or anything in general?

•

I've come here to drink beer and pick up girls, and they're out of beer . . . .

•

I'm not a bad guy, but I'm probably one of the baddest good guys you'll ever meet.

•

I'm the one your mother warned you about.

•

You dig me, except you don't know it yet.

•

Trust me, I'm not a lawyer.

•

Hi! I'm a free agent looking for a new contract.

•

You're hot to trot. Let's tango!

•

Why don't we sweat together?

•

Let's get together this week ... Your gym or mine?

•

Can I wash your workout gear?

•

Hey! You wouldn't want to go skydiving on Saturday by any chance?

•

You are so thin. Do you need someone to take you to dinner?

•

If you're the quarterback, I'm your center.

•

That's a nice dress, how does it come off?

•

Me Tarzan, you Jane.

•

You . . . me . . . now.

•

Astronauts need a rocket to go to the moon, tonight you have me.

•

Do you find anything about me remotely attractive?

•

Darling, you are prettier than my first bicycle!

Lawyers

Somebody's got to defend the juris doctors. Lately, they've gotten a bum rap. But what do you expect? They're an easy target, they're highly visible. Some of these folks have indeed earned their rapscallion reputation for their lawsuit mania, but the rest are decent, hardworking members of society with a little Latin under their belt. Sling a few ipso factos and quid pro quos around and see how quickly you'll be envied, misunderstood, and detested by the masses. Of course the first time you win a landmark case that changes the law, watch how suddenly you'll go from reprehensible to remarkable. It doesn't faze a lawyer—she gets a taste of the whole gamut of humans, from the sublime to the ridiculous—it's business as usual! Thank heaven for evening cocktails and the unbottled spirits sitting at the bar. While some JDs' pick-up lines are a release for pent-up cynicism, others are a celebration of the brighter aspects of humanity.

I'm a lawyer. Want to exchange briefs?

•

Maybe you can help me with an emergency. I need a Tanqueray-Sterling and tonic and a smart woman.

•

I'm strangely attracted to you.

•

You make me went to tell the truth.

•

You are definitely armed, are you dangerous?

•

Girls like you should wear health warnings, "May cause irregular heartbeat."

•

You look like a "Tanqueray" type of guy.

•

That's a lovely set of lungs you're wearing today.

•

If sexy were a crime, you'd be on death row.

•

You're so beautiful, if my eyes were hands, I'd be arrested.

•

Only your intelligence outweighs your looks.

•

Were you my mistress in some past life?

•

You must be an M.D., because you make me feel so good.

•

The walls breathe in anticipation when you walk into the room.

•

What's your name? Is that your real name or your bar name?

•

Used to be a penny for your thoughts. How much will you charge for yours right now?

•

It should be against the law for you to be in public without me.

•

I've got good news for you, I'm taking you out to dinner.

•

If we don't get out of here soon, I'm afraid I may fall in love with you before our first date.

•

If you don't date, how about marriage?

•

Marriage is the only war that allows you to sleep with the enemy.

•

There's never a justice of the peace around when you need one.

•

Would you be interested in a noncommittal, strictly sexual relationship?

•

So what time should I start breakfast in the morning?

•

Hello, dinner.

•

Are you sure you're married?

•

Your lips could be on a glass at my place.

•

I'd even give up my Giant's tickets to spend a Sunday with you.

•

I can bring stability into your destabilized world—let's negotiate.

•

Let's go back to my room and do the things I'm gonna tell my friends we did anyhow.

•

Arrest me, what I'm thinking is criminal!

•

Those you try to snow are never snowed. Those you can snow aren't worth snowing.

•

Frankly, I don't care who makes the first move.

Models

Most people treat them like untouchables because they're so gorgeous or handsome they're intimidating. But they can't help it, they were born that way. The next time you're faced with phenomenal good looks, put yourself in their shoes. Imagine how insecure you'd feel with everyone staring at you. They've just spent their day posing endlessly for photographers on hot and stuffy sets, under blinding lights or out on some equally hot location. Or if they've done the fashion show circuit, they've been walking miles and miles of runways, and turning until it's so automatic it's invaded their dreams at night.

Besides, models are the first to agree that beauty is only skin deep. Long after the first blush fades, it's what's inside that lasts. So what's all the fuss about? They're just as lonely and hungry to connect up as the rest of us. In fact, they're starving for conversation. They may even fumble for words, get tongue-tied, or stutter because the chances are they're a lot more nervous. (Einstein learned to read slowly and couldn't spell well, and his professors thought him a dimwit.) The moral of that reference is never judge a person just based on his or her exterior. Underneath is a mind and a heart that are dying to be noticed by someone. Don't be surprised if Mr. or Ms. Model pays excessive attention to *your* beauty just to break the ice.

What great eyes!

•

Is modeling as much work as it looks?

•

Do you know what time it is?

•

You wouldn't have a cigarette, would you?

•

You probably recognize me from my
underwear ads.

You're very beautiful. . . . Would you share your beauty with me?

•

I'm not rich, but I'm famous among my friends.

•

Nothing tastes as good as you look.

•

You mean you haven't modeled before?

•

My mom warned me about guys like you, but I don't care.

•

I've got the perfect champagne for that outfit back at my place.

•

I love the smell of your leather jacket.

·

I like my vodka straight, like I like my men.

·

I think I could spend the rest of my life with you . . . . or at least the rest of the night.

·

This is not a line but I really think you are beautiful.

·

If I could be a girl for one day, I'd want to look like just like you.

·

The sun turns pale at your smile.

·

You probably recognize me from my underwear ads.

•

Yes, I admit it, I was in your dreams last night.

•

Am I your type?

•

I make great pancakes.

•

No, really, I am thinking of becoming a priest.

•

They said finding the right man would be difficult, but nobody ever said it would be this tough!

•

Aren't you a model or exotic dancer?

•

I'm trying to find a boyfriend for my sister.

•

Tanqueray! Good choice ...

•

Look, it's Elvis!

•

Only visiting this planet.

•

So how tall are you anyway?

•

I'd like to pick you up but I don't think I can.

•

Your eyes are mesmerizing me.

•

Your smile could sell a half million magazine covers.

•

Is it wrong for a woman to want a boy toy?

•

Yes, these are my real breasts.

•

What part of "no" don't you understand?

Nurses

The Florence and Floyd Nightingales of the world bear tremendous responsibility for people whose connection to life is fragile. It's not only a question of monitoring a patient's vital signs and administering medication at the proper interval, nurses are *the* healing presence that mean the difference between hope or futility. And it's not just one patient, but ten, fifteen, twenty patients they have to look after in the course of a day.

What does a nurse do when she or he is feeling saddened or depressed in their own personal lives? When they have their own private pain to deal with? When they're needing someone to take care of them? They can't just tell the hospital to wing it, throw caution to the wind, and go on a day cruise. And they won't because they know they're too important, as the guardians and the givers of life. So, they summon all their strength from the deepest reservoirs of compassion and kindness. Leaving their own battles behind, they march off to win major victories for others in greater need. And in the process, reinforce their own hold on life.

But at the end of the day, you don't expect these warriors of the spirit to go quietly into the night. They will do what any righteous conqueror would do to celebrate the life force. Who needs a flourish of trumpets when the sound of their infectious laughter is loud enough to herald an evening of fun? After you've faced the boundary between life and what lies beyond— and nurses do it every day—the rest of life is a piece of cake. And their pick-up lines reflect that.

Sorry for standing so close, but I seem to be allergic to everyone here except you.

•

We represent the tattoo patrol, and we need to see yours.

•

My, what a beautiful aura you have!

Sorry for standing so close, but I seem to be allergic to everyone here except you.

•

You have the most gorgeous eyelashes I've ever seen on a man.

•

Wow, is that all the "real" you? I mean, all natural, no plastic?

•

Have you seen *Twin Peaks*?

•

What's your IQ? I'm looking for a sperm donor.

•

What is your PH balance?

•

What's the best pressure I should have in my tires?

•

Can I check your heartbeat?

•

You look like you could use a backrub.

•

I've got just what the doctor ordered.

•

I've got to sit down, you're making my knees weak.

•

Could you feel my forehead? I think I'm getting a fever.

•

Why me?

•

I hope you know CPR because you are making my pulse race!

•

Would you like to help me with my physical therapy homework?

•

If I could be anything, I'd like to be your blanket on a cold night.

•

Can I have your mother's number? I want to thank her for bringing you into the world.

•

You were probably a beautiful baby.

•

May I give you a foot massage?

•

You send a chill up my spine—now my posture is better.

•

This place looks so much better when you're in it.

•

You dig me, you just don't know it yet.

•

Will you be the mother of my child.

•

You're hot! Let me be the one to cool you off.

•

Love is the only medicine for a broken heart.

•

You're perfect! The only thing I would change is the sheets.

•

Is your husband married?

•

The only reason you don't recognize me is that I'm the faceless lover in your sexual fantasies.

•

You are definitely the reason I came here tonight.

Office Workers

While everyone else is busting their egos to make it to the top, they're down in the trenches, grinding it out, winning the day-to-day battles, these foot soldiers of corporate America. The backbone, the muscle, and the heartbeat of all business, this country would shut down overnight without them. They keep the machinery oiled and humming at top efficiency. How do they do it? Quite simply with sarcasm. They take themselves lightly. Tomorrow and the day after, and all the days thereafter, they've got to be ready to handle the flack that comes hailing down from above. They've got to bear all the mercurial whims and fluctuating moods, the barometric pressure of their bosses. What's their secret? They're smart, they've conquered their inner wilderness a long time ago. They've learned to transcend. They've gone on to develop a vast reservoir of humor, a sense of levity—otherwise life is an occupational hazard. But do they take the art of pick-up seriously? Not really. That's probably the reason why they have more fun at it, and why they probably dish out some of the funniest pick-up lines.

Hello seems a good start to me.

•

If you don't know me, you're welcome to fill out an application.

•

For one ecstatic moment, I thought I knew you.

•

Weren't you in that top-ten music video?

•

Weren't you in my Sex Ed class?

•

I'm sure I've seen you in another film.

•

You have the best knees I have ever seen.

•

If you were a cookie there wouldn't be any crumbs.

•

You look familiar, didn't we go to different schools at the same time?

•

Excuse me, but I believe we were lovers in a previous life. Shouldn't we just pick up where we left off?

•

I'm writing a telephone book . . . . Can I have your number?

•

I'll have a burger, fries, and your number to go.

•

I'm co-dependent, what's your dysfunction?

•

I'm not looking for Mr. Right, I'm looking for Mr. Right-Now.

•

I've been meaning to call you but I just realized I don't have your number.

•

Wanna come up and see my ferrets?

•

I'm going to a wedding, would you like to come with me and be my bride?

•

Yes, these are two Springsteen first row tickets, all access passes to the party.

•

You know, I think pick-up lines are really immature and demeaning. Would you mind if I just introduce myself?

•

Your place, not mine.

•

Your father told me to take you home.

•

Doesn't someone know you from somewhere?

•

I don't have any etchings, but would you like to come up anyway?

•

I'm really not interested in sex.

•

I don't mean to be forward but how do you like your eggs in the morning?

•

I'm starting early for the next U.S. Census.

•

I'm the designated driver. Can I take you home with me?

•

I've lost my phone number. Can I have yours?

•

If I could only find a friend who means as much to me as I mean to them.

•

Would you be requiring anything else but my presence?

Photographers

They're the ones sitting at the bar who are anything but still, drinking in the peoplescape, mixing the palette in their mind's eye, excited by their most current assignment—the possibilities are as rich as their imaginations. Not unlike bakers, photographers are given the same ingredients to work with, and yet their end results are all different. Indeed, the photographer is a highly subjective artist. An obvious truth, yes, but highly inflammatory. People are actually still debating whether photography is an art! After all, say the opponents, a photographer is only pressing a button to give you an exact duplication of nature. Where's the art? It's in the photographer's eye, a very personal eye, which is the window to a very particular soul. Anytime you train your eye on some aspect of life you start to "get under the skin of it." You begin to feel for your subject, you bridge a connection, and thus begins understanding. Images tell stories and the perspective on those images reveals the photographer's feelings about life.

Anyone who's had the good luck to sit next to a still-life photographer agrees there a certain agility to their approach, a certain liveliness that stems from their love affair with truth as beauty. A photographer's #1 rule: there are no rules! With that in mind, expect a little worship and the unexpected to spring from their lips.

Are you following me?

•

Hi, my name is ———. I'm tired of all this male bonding around here. How about a drink?

•

Didn't I see you squeezing melons at the market earlier this evening?

•

Let's go, I hate being recognized— by the bartender.

•

It's so crowded and noisy in here, maybe we should go to the phone booth so we can talk in peace?

•

Excuse me, is that face taken?

•

I could have sworn you were that gorgeous swimsuit model.

•

Miss Tanqueray, I presume!

•

Weren't you on the cover of *Cosmo* last month?

•

Ninety-five percent of the women in here would kill to look like you.

•

Were you born in those jeans?

•

You make magazine models look sickly!

•

You're an actress, aren't you?

•

If I could be the tear—to be born in your eye, live on your cheek, and die on your lips.

•

Where did you get that nice mouth?

•

I've got a great puppy at home that would love to meet you.

•

Love your smile.

•

You have the coolest freckles I've ever seen.

•

You have the most beautiful eyes in the world, and I'd like to celebrate this point with you.

•

Is it the light in here or are you really an angel?

•

We must be on the *Enterprise* because your face just beamed me up.

•

You look just like a Nagel print come to life. Do you want to stop by my place and see the one I mean?

•

You know, I'm actually Elvis's clone!

•

Pardon me for staring, but you are art to me.

•

So is that a short leather skirt you're wearing or just a wide belt?

•

Lets go to the darkroom and see what develops.

•

Our children would be gorgeous!

•

I could make you famous.

•

It's been a slice, can I have a piece?

•

I hope you like Pop-Tarts . . . because that's what we're having for breakfast.

Physicists

No, you say, when does a physicist have time to be a regular person? With all that calculus swimming around in their heads, a lounge would be the last place you'd expect to find a physicist. Not according to bartenders. In fact, the late Richard Feynman, one of the most eccentric of the breed, used to hang out in bars because he genuinely loved the caprices of fellow human beings; it was an excuse to give vent to his own fickle nature.

Okay, so the average physicist spends his or her days in mathematical dimensions beyond most people's comprehension. But they're still flesh and blood, and they still have appetites. So toss out any preconceived notions about them (and stop yawning). Once you get a physicist away from the lab, they're far from being pompous or boring. They're more like the Mad Hatter, but sexier. It's a fact, a stimulated mind is the greatest aphrodisiac. Besides, quarks, gravity, and antimatter may be fascinating stuff, but there is nothing more mysterious than a human being. (Physicists know it better than anyone else.) And there is nothing more whimsical, even goofy, than physicists who enjoy the lively men and women they are. Their pick-up lines are proof positive!

Excuse me, I am not from this area. Could you please tell me where you live?

•

You are living proof! There is a God!

•

So you're the one responsible for the earthquake last night.

•

I've been wondering what you were going to look like.

•

Didn't we share the same nursery room?

·

Want to come over for milk and cookies?

·

I'm in love with you. I'm only mildly maladjusted.

·

You can sit there, but promise not to talk about the weather.

·

You have the most interesting ears I've ever seen.

·

You couldn't care less about the ban on silicon, right?

·

Is there a model convention in town?

·

We have to leave now, there's going to be a raid.

•

You're causing a nuclear reaction in my heart.

•

I could feel your energy across the room.

•

The world has so many wonders and you are one, my love.

•

How do they determine whether a species such as you is endangered or extinct?

•

I'd like to get your phone number as soon as possible because my parole officer is due here to pick me up any minute.

·

Let's get married tonight!

·

Don't reason, just come home with me!

·

We can be like two dice and roll the odds.

·

Would you mind helping me bridge the gap between adolescence and senility?

·

What's a good spaghetti sauce?

·

I'm really not interested in sex.

·

Our genes were meant to splice together.

•

Can I play in your sandbox?

•

Excuse me, but why do I get the feeling that we once cohabited the same space in a parallel universe?

•

Check your pocket, I think you've stolen my heart.

•

Did you know that in Greek your name means "vision of loveliness"?

•

What took our paths so long to cross?

•

If you were in my dreams, I'd sleep forever.

Politicians

Regardless of what side they're on, all deserve an A for effort. Speaking of which, the energy of one politician alone could possibly keep a power station humming for a year.

It takes sheer bravado to thrust yourself into the public eye, to subject yourself to such intense scrutiny—microbes get better treatment. Grace under pressure is the creed of every politician who must walk a tightrope between opposing forces. But grace alone will not get them elected. They need a certain amount of charisma that magnetizes people to them like iron filings. After the grace and the charisma, then they've got to deliver the goods like a pro salesman. And that's where the boys get separated from the men, the girls from the women. Sure, they have their assistants to help with the workload, but they also have to be quick studies—there's no other way they can handle the landslide of information. Keeping up with ordinances, bills, and amendments is only a fraction of the job; the art of persuasion makes up the other nine-tenths, from coaxing their colleagues and cajoling their foes in government, to galvanizing their constituents back home for the next round. The best politicians are the best salesmen in the world and vice versa. As a man or a woman for all seasons, a politician knows they must look for a win-win situation for everyone, *especially* at the bar:

Hi, I'm saving this stool for the best-looking girl in the place. Would you like to sit down?

•

Wasn't it you who liked to play post office after the Howdy Doody Show ended?

•

So ... do you think the U.S. will ever convert to liters, from pints and ounces?

•

Do you know my brother—he comes in here all the time. No?

Well do you mind if I sit with you till he comes?

•

I'm only wearing these sunglasses because I'm blinded by your beauty.

•

I didn't know that angels flew so close to the ground.

•

Haven't I seen you in my wildest dreams?

•

You remind me of a love I once knew, is this real or is it déjà vu?

•

Of all the women I've met, you are definitely one of them.

•

I'm only wearing these sunglasses because I'm blinded by your beauty.

So which rock star stamp did you vote for?

•

Funny, you don't look like a Republican.

•

That's the nicest pair of . . . jeans I've seen in a long time.

•

So you're the reason people believe in love at first sight.

•

Do you have a map? I'm lost inside your eyes and can't find my way out.

•

Last film do well?

•

Do your plans for tonight include me?

•

Could I have my heart back now or do you enjoy having stolen merchandise in your possession?

•

The essence of your being has affected my ability to bowl.

•

You are too good to be true.

•

If you were a magazine, I'd subscribe.

•

Now that I've met you my life finally has meaning.

•

Pardon me, are you busy for the next 60 years?

•

I'm looking for a good home for my dog. Do you have one?

•

Excuse me, I was just about ready to leave when I realized I forgot something—you!

•

Isn't this place dead? I think you and I are the caretakers and don't know it.

•

Want to see where the horse bit me?

•

Can we play doctor or nurse? I need intensive care.

•

Lifestyles of the poor and crazy, that's where I come in.

Psychologists

According to some of our bartender sources, their psychologist customers run the gamut from those who liked to box people into different categories, to those who *depended* upon their bartender for wisdom, to those who refused to judge or label anyone, claiming the best compass in life is what one *prefers*.

"Different crop of head doctors coming up today," said one bartender in Brentwood, California, shaking his head. "I thought I understood them but they've gone and changed on me." When pressed as to how they've changed, he had to take a moment to answer. "They're not out to psych everyone out anymore." At least the good ones aren't. They have hang-ups like the rest of us; they're not afraid to admit it because they're not on any ego trip. They just happen to make their living understanding people and helping them.

"But what if you can't afford hundreds of

dollars in therapy?" One person we surveyed asked a man who practiced counseling at the local hospital. "Then give yourself plenty of love," he replied. In one simple statement, he demystified *getting well*. He, incidentally, was one of the therapists unwilling to judge, who are out there socializing with real people, having real fun, throwing out real pick-up lines.

What did you want to be when you were a kid?

•

This may seem trite, but haven't we met?

•

Are you in therapy?

•

Weren't we married in the '70s?

•

Who was that masked man?

•

Hello, I guess I don't know you from anywhere.

•

Are you real, or am I dreaming?

•

I'm sorry, I don't remember you from a past life.

•

I'm a doctor and I feel a responsibility to tell you you've got a serious case of the cutes.

•

Would you thank your parents for me?

•

Hi, I'm a psychology major. Care to be scrutinized?

•

Darling, you are prettier than my first bicycle.

•

Would you please tell me how it feels to be that beautiful?

•

I had a vision I'd meet someone like you tonight.

•

You look like a hell of a guy!

•

We were destined to meet.

•

So, do you want to have a life?

•

Love is best when shared by two.

•

You remind me of my mother.

•

Love me or hate me, but spare me your indifference.

•

You're gorgeous and I'm married. Life can be so unfair.

•

This too shall pass.

•

Smile, it can't be that bad.

•

Your smile makes the night as bright as daylight.

•

Don't you hate pick-up lines?

•

My goodness gracious, I'd like you to be a part of my personal life.

•

We seem to speak the same unspoken language fluently, don't you think?

•

It might work if we went to therapy together.

•

Pardon me, are you enjoying your life, or was the last one better?

•

Mom!? What are you doing here?

•

Should all else fail, we can be friends.

Radio Announcers

The voice floats above all the others at the bar. It's so modulated it oozes honey, the tempo so regulated you can almost hear the metronome beating in the background. But the most distinctive feature about announcers is they're able to laugh at themselves. When you do radio six hours a day, six days a week, you *are* the station. On top of all that, disk jockeys are expected to be amusing spontaneously. And if they commit a blooper, guess what? it sails out into the airwaves to thousands of listeners. No luxury of failing in the privacy of their own cubbyholes. But not even the risk of public humiliation can deter them. Some hang in there thirty or forty years, a testament to their steel-belted nerves.

So what makes them tick? There has to be something behind people who psyche themselves up to put on a perfect show every day; who walk the gauntlet for a living. According to the bartenders interviewed, there's a whole lot of cynicism behind these folks. For every cheery sound that emanates from their mouths, there's a parallel thought so dry and brilliant, it would challenge *The Best of Saturday Night Live*. It shouldn't be a secret to anyone, though, because if you close your eyes and listen to the quality of a person's voice you can hear the depth of intelligence. And there's plenty of that echoing throughout the following pick-up lines.

That voice! Aren't you the wrong number that I dialed last night?

•

Excuse me, didn't our paths cross during the last solar eclipse?

•

Hi, I'm the devil and it's not your soul I want.

•

So we meet again! Isn't reincarnation great!

•

Incredible! I didn't know you would be here.

•

Is your seat taken?

•

I feel an outbreak of Magnetic Attraction Syndrome coming on.

•

Do you want to see my streetcar named Desire?

•

Say, didn't we meet at my first wedding?

•

I'm looking for a pleaser, not a teaser.

•

It's annual pick-up time.

•

The Lord is my Shepherd, I see what I want.

•

Can I interest you in some counter indoctrination?

•

I like your accent, pure South Milwaukee.

•

Your skin looks so soft, you must bathe every day.

•

If smiles were dollars, you'd be a millionaire.

•

Forgive me for staring, but I draw classical nudes.

•

How many drinks would I have to buy you to make me look good?

•

I'm cooking chicken, do you wanna neck?

•

Pass the bread, here comes the baloney.

•

I'm not easy, but we can talk about it.

•

I'm warm for your form.

•

How about a large pizza and a small booth?

•

Would you like to see my Desert Storm medals?

•

Even if your answer is no, nod your head yes so I don't look stupid.

•

Throwing a wedding bouquet is like throwing a hand grenade.

•

You have a great body. Can I try it on for size?

•

Can I do your laundry?

•

Don't let the gray hair fool you—I live in the fast lane and I'm only 25.

•

It's time to do everything you wanted to do and didn't want to do.

•

There isn't a desert I wouldn't cross for your phone number.

•

I'm hungry for love, so set the table.

•

Are there any more at home like you?

•

You molten mass of manhood . . .
make me a woman tonight!

•

I'd love to rock your world.

•

My mother warned me to stay away
from women like you. Then again,
I never listened to Mom.

•

Hey, pretty lady, that beautiful
smile just brightened my day.

•

Next to being born, you're the best
thing that's happened to me!

•

Nice boots. Are they hard to get off?

•

I'm your knight in shining armor.
Let's get medieval.

•

I'd love to be the Prince Charming
who wakes you up in the morning.

•

You would be so much more
attractive without a wedding ring.

•

Why is it that men get dogs for best
friends and women get diamonds?

Reporters

They're always on the run for the next big story. The one that may land them a Pulitzer. Because they're not just reporting, they're investigating, and in a lot of cases blowing the lid off the real story. With minds like steel traps, they'll seize on a microscopic detail, some little discrepancy, and dig and dig until they've unearthed the whole animal. They're a healthy combination of sleuth and psychologist with the added duties of a writer under deadline. But they love the pressure, the chase, the adrenaline rush; they crave it like some people crave chocolate, and wouldn't have it any other way.

They're really not the hard-boiled cynics that you think. In between, during the "quiet" times, Mr. or Ms. Reporter can be found at a favorite watering hole wrapped around a double Tanqueray-Sterling martini on the rocks, asking the same question we're all asking . . . "what's it all about?" They're really very sensitive underneath, very sensual, and very funny (sometimes wickedly so)—their pick-up lines are the telltale signs.

Nice dress, can I talk you out of it?

•

Let me buy you a drink and we can tell each other lies.

•

I work for Student Affairs. Would you like to have one?

•

Excuse me, but why do I get the feeling that we once covered the same story in another life?

•

I'd like to introduce you to a kind, sensitive, passionate, sexy guy . . . me.

•

After seeing you in your college sweatshirt, I immediately began lusting after your mind.

•

You make me crazy, baby!

•

Just looking at you makes me crave a cigarette.

•

So, what's a nice girl like you doing in a fantasy like mine?

•

Why would a beautiful girl like you dye the roots of her hair brown?

•

Was that you who left the provocative message on my answering machine the other night?

•

Is it windy, or am I just breathing hard?

•

Dial 911, my heart has stopped!

•

I have a question, but don't answer me till morning.

•

I'd like to see you in the morning, should I call or just roll over?

•

You have no idea how good your chances are, with me.

•

You're so hot, you make the devil sweat.

•

Care to engage in some primitive humanoid behavior patterns?

•

Let's go sledding in my bathtub.

•

I believe that the body is a temple, would you grant me sanctuary?

•

I'm madly in lust with you.

•

I'd love to be the tonic that soothes your Tanqueray-Sterling.

•

We have to leave now—there's going to be a raid.

•

If I followed you home would you keep me?

•

Where do I take a number and stand in line to make an appointment to worship you?

•

Hey, come back here! I'm not done looking at you yet!

•

Hurricane Andrew would stop dead in his tracks if he saw you.

•

An idle mind is the devil's workshop, so let's get busy.

•

What did you say your phone number was?

•

I know we've never met, but I can't seem to forget you. . .

•

My mother told me you'd be here.

Researchers

She's just gotten back from one in thousands of fantastic journeys she will take in her life. The microscope gives her passage into the interior worlds of life forms vast and foreign to the human eye. And when a researcher returns from such a journey, nothing's quite the same about his own reality anymore. It all seems so different, especially sitting at the bar now and looking at all the human life around him. It's curious that the deeper one goes into the infinitesimal, the greater the perspective one gets on all life. The mundane doesn't seem ordinary, quite so much as it seems miraculous. The real magic is not illusion. It lies in the fact there is so much balance and symmetry in life; that nature has order, rhythm, and harmony. It's this very observation that gives the researcher tremendous affection for all that surrounds him. It's hard for them to be critical of anyone or anything when they're awestruck by the intelligence that invests all life, from the amoeba to the human being. You'll be able to spot them immediately by their dialogue—there's no excess verbiage. Nothing's forced or manufactured about their words. No need to dance around the truth. If they like you, you'll know it. They say just what their heart prompts—how can you improve upon honesty like the following?

Tell me, how can a drink that advertises 100 percent spring water, have at least 10 percent fruit juice?

•

Something compelled me to walk over to you and say hello.

•

Weren't you in the incubator next to me in 1966?

•

Was that you on cable T.V.?

•

What do you do in the real world?

•

You intrigue me.

•

I'm shy, you're beautiful, may I buy
you a drink?

•

I'm never going to see you again,
but I want you to know I think
you're adorable.

•

You look like my dream invader.

•

You have the most beautiful feet.

•

I don't mean to seem forward, but can we talk?

•

Do you have a piece of gum?

•

I've been out of circulation lately. Can you help pull me back in?

•

So you're the reason I've been alone so long.

•

Do you have something in your eye, or did you blink at me?

•

No, I'm not shy, my tongue has been surgically removed.

•

Would you like some company?

•

So when are we going out?

•

Your glow warms me.

•

Let's sow wild oats tonight and pray for crop failure tomorrow!

•

You are very well put together.

•

Standing here, looking at you, has strengthened my knowledge of perfection!

•

(Toward the end of the evening) Your legs must be really tired 'cause you've been running through my mind all night.

•

You look more beautiful than the last time I saw you.

•

Wow, you're breathtaking.

•

Today's my birthday. Would you like to celebrate with me?

•

Ever wonder where we would be if sex were an unpleasant experience?

•

Wherever you're going, they will be blessed to have your presence.

•

What time would you like me to pick you up on Saturday?

Sailors

Gentle and sweet but hardy of constitution and spirit, they worship the sea and the wind. Their devotion is so strong, it reminds you of a marriage. They take the stormy times with the calmer, even-tempered moments, cursing the former and cherishing the latter. Some are independently wealthy, others are just frugal expatriates of the land.

Every so often they'll go on furlough and check into port, a token nod to civilization. They won't stay long, they get antsy for their "mate," who undulates them to sleep and who by morning can turn on them like a beast. No matter, they like the challenge, they crave the danger, it takes them to the edge of life, tests their invincibility. But behind the weary, weather-worn exterior is a Huck (or Holly) Finn born to run wild. They've docked for one reason—they're hunger for a little human warmth. They'll tell you about the time a wind

came up out of the east and nearly capsized the
boat while a school of sharks was circling their
boat. Or the time they were on their way to
Tahiti and were nearly done in by a freak hurricane. But first they'll throw out a pick-up line
that may either sound like it came from a child
or a fearless and wizened Father Time. You be
the judge.

You're back! I thought you were in
Bora Bora. For Godsakes, give me
a hug!

•

Finally, a dreamboat among so
many shipwrecks.

•

You look just like my first wife . . .
and I've never been married.

•

I already love you, now what's your
name?

•

I come here in the mating season, and you?

.

Am I in a museum or are you just one fine piece of art?

.

Is everyone else really boring or are you just exciting?

.

I'm all real, are you?

.

Of all the peaches in the world, you're a plum.

.

If you cook as good as you look, I'll eat the bottom of the pot.

.

You look just like the Mona Lisa's younger sister.

•

Somewhere between thirty and death.

•

Were you on the *Ecstasy*, cruising in the Caribbean not too long ago?

•

Your eyes could steal a sailor from the sea.

•

You're the star I wished upon last night.

•

If you think this Tanqueray-Sterling Vodka is great, you should taste the bottle I have at my place!

•

Pardon me, have you ever had sex on the beach?

•

If I were a race horse, I'd love for you to be my jockey.

•

Would you like to come over to my house for a nap on my waterbed?

•

How would you like to come up to my room and see my fish tank?

•

I'm built for comfort, not for speed.

•

It's not the size of the boat, it's the motion of the ocean.

•

If I could hold the hands I love, I'd be holding yours.

•

Excuse me, but are you an angel?

•

Let's fall in love for the night.

•

I could be your mother's worst nightmare and make your dreams come true.

•

You don't dance like you're from the suburbs.

•

Let me take you away from this.

•

I don't follow women into bars, so I'm glad you're already here.

•

Your castle or mine.

Stockbrokers

They'll play mental chess and checkmate you if you aren't on top of things. They pride themselves on being able to forecast the financial weather. And the best are not too far off target. Thousands of their clients' dollars ride on their prophesies. It wouldn't take long for the most humble amongst us to get a heady feeling from all that real or imagined power. But then nature is the great equalizer. She runs around trimming everyone's sense of self-importance. One day's plunge in the stock market can put an ego on a crash diet, bring you to your knees. Advising investors large and small can thrust you into a permanent state of anxiousness or panic. It's a risky seesaw—about as stable as mercury. But stockbrokers learn to trust that the most predictable thing about the world is its unpredictability. Hedging on inflation is one thing, hedging on rejection is a second cousin. But then again, some stockbrokers are bullish, and others bearish. You'll see from the diversity of pick-up lines below.

Hi, I'm rich!

•

This is your lucky day.

•

I've noticed you looking my way, is it me or the guy next to me?

•

So, is your boyfriend as good-looking as I am?

•

Is that your Porsche in front of the building?

•

Wasn't that you tailgating me on Rodeo Drive?

•

You look like the girl in the dream I had last night.

•

What color is your BMW?

•

Your eyes are suggestive.

•

Didn't we share the chair lift at St. Moritz last winter?

•

There's Noooooo question about it, you bought that body!

•

Do you have a license to display such beauty?

•

You're the most beautiful woman in

this room and we'd make great babies.

•

Nice legs, nice body, nice lady— can I buy you a drink?

•

When you walk, you've got more moves than a Swiss watch.

•

If I thought a pick-up line would work, I'd use one right now.

•

Do you wanna get to know me? Be honest!

•

My favorite color is leather. What's yours?

•

Nice Dress! It would look great on the floor next to my bed!

•

Hey, babe! Take a walk on the wild side.

•

Is that smile patented?

•

Want to trade fax numbers?

•

I'd love to be the seam on your pants.

•

There's no way I'd leave a gorgeous girl like you sitting alone.

•

I'm going home now. Want to go with me?

•

You don't need a palm reader or a psychic to see that I'm in your future.

•

What's your name and number? I'd like to call you to make plans for marriage.

•

I don't have much time—will you marry me?

•

Try the best. Try *me*.

•

Excuse me, I seem to have lost the keys to my Lamborghini, did you happen to pick them up?

•

Don't waste your quarter, use my car phone.

Traveling Salesmen
or Women

After being cooped up in a car all day long in bumper-to-bumper traffic, the salesman or woman is ready to party when they hit the watering hole. Now if they've just landed a new account, you might see them hang from the chandeliers in celebration. Or if there are only overhead spotlights in the night club, they're probably settle for buying a round of drinks for everyone at the bar.

Their minds now humming at optimum speed from sharing their victories, they're ready and willing to listen to you. The best people in sales are the most compassionate. They make great advisors because they're driven to find solutions to every problem. In fact if you ask a salesman or woman, there *are* no problems. Everything is strictly a challenge. They've spent countless hours psyching themselves up for success.

They've visualized it, they've hypnotized themselves for it, and absolutely nothing will stop them from achieving it. Which is refreshing because they're a positive source of energy. Consider yourself lucky if you're sitting next to them at the bar, some of those winning vibes may rub off onto you. They won't ply you with elaborate set-ups just to get a response out of you. They're simple and direct. But don't be surprised if they don't give up, if first they don't succeed . . .

You! I know you!

•

Since you're already in my seat, let me introduce you to its owner.

•

My middle name is Potential.

•

I understand you wanted to meet me!

•

I'm from the Hotel & Sales & Marketing Association, and someday you'll pay to sleep with me!

•

When you smile, you light up the whole room.

•

Where'd you get that million-dollar smile?

•

Has anyone ever told you your mother has the most beautiful daughter?

•

The word "stunning" doesn't even come close to describing you.

•

When God created you, He made no mistakes!

•

May I please stand next to you because you brighten up my world.

•

May I be the olive in your martini?

•

I never have a drink unless I'm with someone or alone.

•

Just because I'm on a diet doesn't mean I can't look at the menu.

•

You know, I could get sugar diabetes loving someone as sweet as you.

•

Too much of a good thing is wonderful.

•

I'm new in town, could you show me the sights?

•

And someone divorced you?

•

You may not know this but you're my future wife.

•

Would you believe I'm a hotdog salesman?

•

It's now or never!

•

Can I be your friend?

•

Can I drive you home?

•

Be positive, say you will have dinner.

•

You are the hottest thing since sunburn.

•

Did you know I'm separated?

•

I haven't got a phone, but you can reach out and touch me.

•

[After splashing water] I think I should take you home and get you out of these wet clothes.

•

I just want to tell you, you have completely made my day.

•

So when do you have to be back in heaven?

•

I'm your knight in shining armor. Let's get medieval.

Excuse me, but I just can't help noticing your eyes. I love the way they've been all over me since I walked in here.

•

I love your socks! [Best used when the other person isn't wearing socks.]

•

Didn't we have anonymous phone sex last night?

•

Aren't you my future ex-husband?

•

Which is easier? Getting into those pants or getting out of them?

•

You look familiar to me. Are you by chance from Oklahoma?

Waiters

Most have hot feet (or at least a pair of invisible wings that strap onto their ankles). But moving fast is only one of the requirements for success in this job. Remembering orders, faces, names is another, not to mention speed in math, smiling on cue, dispensing empathy where needed, and above all else, controlling one's temper. As with any service job, you must stock up on diplomacy—especially when the Loud party of six arrives, just as the Whiner party of five starts complaining. Opposite the Contentious table of two who are quarreling. After an eight-hour shift, some rightfully collapse, while others can take on the world—they're revved and ready to brandish their wit.

Is there a sign on my chest that says over 10 billion served?

•

Frankly, I don't care who makes the first move.

•

How would you like your eggs?

•

I'm really much better-looking than this—I just don't like drawing attention to myself at work.

•

If I am bread, would you be my butter?

•

You're the best-looking dish I've seen since supper.

•

I caught a fever when you walked in the room.

•

I could not resist telling you how irresistible you are.

•

You just popped my contacts.

•

You look like my second husband. How many times have you been married?

•

If you are employed, I'm single.

•

Is that drink for me?

•

Weren't you the Lotto winner last week?

•

With my looks and your money we could really go places together.

•

You look like you could use something bubbly—me.

•

I know that I don't work here but can I help you anyway?

•

The management has designated me to be your date tonight.

•

It's not pretty being easy.

•

I think it would be so nice just to pour you over ice and sip slowly.

•

What's that perfume you're wearing? Catch of the day?

•

Could it be magic or amusement?

•

If you want some companionship, why don't you just ask?

•

You look very sexy tonight, can we talk?

•

Mi casa or su casa?

•

Do you speak English? Oh, good so do I.

•

If I don't find someone I like and marry her by next Friday, I'll lose a huge inheritance. Would you like to dance?

•

I cannot handle rejection.

•

Yes, I'm the one who lost the glass slipper last night.

•

What's your sign? Mine's Yield.

•

Isn't your family with the circus?

•

You look so different with your clothes on!

•

Gosh, your hair smells great!

•

We could share brushes.

•

Can I borrow you for the night?

•

With a tongue like that, who needs ice cream?

•

Would you deny a dying man's last wish?

•

It must be karma . . . or was it Carmen??

•

Who does your hair?

•

No, really, I like your hair.

•

Worked for the vice squad long?

•

Love your nails, who does them?

•

If you were in my dreams, I'd sleep forever.

•

I don't see a ring. Are you spoken for?

•

Would you help me with my groceries? Why not carry them . . . cook them?

•

Haven't you picked me up before?

•

I am just another brilliant mind ruined by education.

Writers

If the man or woman next to you nearly apologizes for breathing, chances are he's a member of the writing class. Some of the most humble people on the face of this earth are wordsmiths. Undoubtedly their humility has something to do with all the rejection slips overflowing their wastebasket.

So don't be alarmed if they back into a conversation. Throughout the animal kingdom, posturing defensively is highly valued in terms of survival. All critters, large and small, stand a pretty good chance of not being attacked, at least initially. The signal is unmistakable: "I'd like to know you: I will not harm you." Once they've got your attention with the humble remark, writers will trot out clever lines like brand-new toys. They'll do it just to hear your laughter—a most powerful elixir that a) turns a brooding wordsmith into a fountain of joy, and b) tells him he's worthy even though his manuscripts are ignored, and c) reminds him life's worth living after all. Now if the word-smith happens to get lucky and end up charming you into a date, there's no telling what sort of wordplay he or she has in store for you.

I couldn't help notice you were ignoring me.

•

Pardon me, but do you happen to know who I am?

•

I'm compiling an independent telephone directory. You wouldn't want to be left out, would you?

•

Before this life, wasn't I your favorite lap dog?

•

Wasn't I married to you?

•

Would it be possible to sit at your feet and beg?

•

You remind me a lot of my mother.

•

Judging from the cover, I'd love to read the book.

•

Your eyes speak volumes to me.

•

I may not remember your name, but I'll never forget your pupils.

•

When are we going to get to the good part?

•

Have you conjugated any good verbs lately?

•

I think I bought a case of Girl Scout cookies from you once.

•

You make me feel like a schoolboy in love for the first time.

•

You might think I'm drunk, but I'm just intoxicated by your beauty.

•

If I'm not having a heart attack, then Cupid just struck me.

•

Is that smile patented?

•

I've never seen my type packaged so well.

•

Either you or a microwave is messing up my pacemaker.

•

My name is ———. Remember it, because you'll be thinking about it all night.

•

A good man is hard to find, a hard man is good to find.

•

What is the sexiest man in America doing in this bar?

•

Stop the contest, we've found a winner.

•

Would you like a drink? Sure. Well, then get me one while you're at it.

•

There's something about you I like.
I just can't put my finger on it.

•

They're not both yours, are they?

•

Whoa! You gorgeous hunk of man,
I'll be here again tomorrow. See ya.

•

My friends say the sex change was
a success—what do you think?

•

At no time will my hands leave my
wrists.

•

I'm writing a new novel and I'd like
to model my heroine after you.

•

What perfume are you wearing? I think it's the same perfume as a character in my novel.

•

But will you still love me in the morning?

•

You really should talk to me someday. We could be married.

•

If I gave you roses, would you give me two-lips?

•

You have a boyfriend? Good, he can pay for the parking.

•

Actually my mother-in-law and I have a lot in common, we both wish my wife had married someone else.

•

Hurry up and give me your number before I don't want it anymore.

•

How about a bite?

•

I'm writing a book on opening lines. What would work with you?

•

Keep me, I may be valuable someday.

A Line for
Every Occasion

Some lines resound across the board without regard to the career of the person saying them. It matters not whether the speaker is an accountant or a waiter, there are certain themes that recur in all minds as in all great art. As their effect upon people is most persuasive and therefore powerful, we thought they deserved special attention:

The Compliment
The Offer
The Innuendo

The Compliment

The quickest way to sell yourself to someone is to throw a compliment his way. It reflects on your good taste, ample enough to recognize his quality. According to the bartenders and consumers we spoke to, it's the number one type of pick-up line that's used throughout bars in America. For good reason: it succeeds over and over again. Whether it's half-baked or overblown, it still works magic with most bipeds, and almost all quadripeds. Pure, old-fashioned positive energy turns the wattage up in a person. Even if you're sitting next to someone with a moat and drawbridge around her personality, it's still the shortest possible distance to her heart. In fact, a lot of bartenders have witnessed miracles in the presence of a compliment.

One regular, a fairly appealing guy on any other day, walked into his favorite watering hole in Manhattan. He had had a particularly bad day. By his fifth beer, he was unloading a dumpster of problems on the bartender. Most of the patrons nearly got fed up, downed a quick drink, and left. In walks an elfish type. Seemingly oblivious to the toxins gushing from his mouth, she loudly proclaimed, "There should be a law against all that beauty!" It stopped him cold. "What beauty?" he asked. "Yours," she said. He gave an embarrassed laugh and just sat there, speechless. She'd switched channels on him; it took him a while to get his bearings. But when he came back from being dislocated, he was downright charming. They exchanged numbers by the end of the night. Six months later they were engaged.

Though most compliments are not that dramatically mood-altering, they still carry tremendous impact. Here are some of the winners.

Hi! You look clean.

•

You look like my cat, warm and cuddly.

•

You intrigue me.

•

Baby, you've got more legs than a bucket of chicken.

•

Standing here next to you, I believe I've died and gone to heaven.

•

You have a lovely body.

•

Getting close to you wouldn't be close enough.

•

Wasn't that you in my dreams last night?

•

When you get up in the morning, the sun has a reason to shine.

•

You raise my consciousness.

•

Thank you for being so perfect.

•

You have fascinating eyes! Can I buy you a drink?

•

You have the type of chest the gods ate olives off of.

Baby, you've got more legs than a
bucket of chicken.

•

You're like a cool summer breeze.

•

Did you realize you were the most beautiful woman here?

•

Would it be politically correct to tell you how beautiful you are?

•

You are the standard of excellence to be equaled or surpassed here tonight.

•

Whatever you're doing, it's working.

•

Weren't you on the cover of Vogue?

•

Somebody must have opened the doors to paradise.

•

You look like a good pool player. . . . Maybe you could show me a few pointers.

•

Mother Nature has been very generous to you.

•

You get better-looking every day.

•

Bartender, check this woman's ID. She looks too young to be in here.

•

That's a great tattoo, who did it?

•

Did Leonardo DaVinci paint you, too?

•

If beauty were measured by the seconds, you'd be an hour.

•

Are you embarrassed to be so beautiful?

•

If I were stranded on an island, I'd only bring this drink and you.

•

You're beautiful when you're angry.

The Offer

Any offer you extend to the stranger next to you to buy them a condo, a jet, a sports car, a trip, jewelry, or even a drink truly warms their heart. Or if not real estate or liquor, the offer of marriage will do. the offer, understood by all, is the common denominator, spoken in a universal tongue, the language of assets (coupled with the promise of romance). Also, like most music, it appeals directly to the emotions. You may think the person next to you at the bar has a dead bolt on their heart. Just mention one word: Ferrari. Amazing, isn't it, how quickly the lock slides open as their eyes light up. Even in jest, because you've provided a temporary escape from the ordinary. They're suddenly transported to a swifter, freer, more powerful life in their imagination. Now if you happen to own a Ferrari, that freedom's a reality. But don't even think about that. With or without the real estate, the greatest asset you own is yourself and your ability to stir another person. No amount of money can come close to you most invaluable asset: a rich imagination.

Now, try making an offer of marriage, if only in jest. It's the nearest and dearest hope, dream, and desire of most single people. Both men and women have a craving for those delicious, wonderful differences between the genders—a craving that can only be satisfied ultimately by uniting with their other half in matrimony.

Take your pick, though, the offers cover a wide gamut.

Hello, I'm rich and I don't believe in prenuptial arrangements.

•

We just came into an inheritance, want to help me spend it?

•

My parents willed me $10 million on the grounds that I marry by the weekend, can I buy you a drink?

•

So, who wants to take my private jet to Paris?

•

Let's go for a spin in my Ferrari.

•

Can I buy you a condo?

•

Couldn't you help me reach the maximum on my credit cards?

•

Can I buy a drink, a ring, a house, a car, what about a key to my heart?

•

Do you eat? I'd like to buy you dinner.

•

Would you like to come back to my place for some vodka and a game of chess?

•

What do you say to breakfast in Paris?

•

Need a ride?

•

Can I buy you a drink or a Mercedes?

•

Want to play house?

•

I'd like to buy you a small house in the country . . . of your choice.

•

Your left hand would look great with a diamond on it.

•

Your place or Tahiti?

•

I could get used to showering you with gifts the rest of our lives.

•

Care to help me spend $10 million? I just won the Lottery!

•

Would you mind holding my keys to my Porsche, just in case I can't drive you home.

•

This is a picture of my son, cute, isn't he? Wanna make one?

•

Wanna come over to my place and study irregular verbal systems?

•

You look thirsty. . . . Can I wet my whistle with your lips?

•

May I join you?

•

How about a game of one on one?

•

Hey, wanna arm wrestle for a quarter?

•

How would you like to save the world together?

•

I would be yours till all the streams run dry.

•

What can I do to you—Oh, I mean for you?

•

I am a massage therapist. Let me show you.

The Innuendo

What's the next best thing to sensual gratification? Talk about it. Just the very mention of a filet mignon will conjure up succulent memories of past mignons, stirring the juices of our salivary glands. The same holds true for the clever, sophisticated, and/or hilarious references to sex. As the richest expression of love between two people, sex is physically, mentally, and spiritually the most satisfying activity on the face of this earth. There is no greater quest in life than our search for a mate, that one special man or woman to bridge the loneliness, to share our emotions with, to add meaning, depth, and dimension to our lives. And when someone sparks our interest, ignites our chemistry, tickles our minds, then hope rises up as invincibly as the morning sun. Just a flicker of possibility of bliss with another person has a magical effect upon our lives, transforming our mood, accelerating our heartbeat, and lubricating our words as they roll from our tongues.

Am I one of the things on your list to pick up today?

•

Wow! Nice pair of . . . shoes!

•

We've met, in my dreams.

•

If I were a motorcycle I would want you to ride me all the time.

•

Looking at something hot like you makes me warm all over.

•

You are so hot, you could melt the fire in my eyes.

•

I'd sure like to see your resumé.

•

If I didn't have this heart condition, I'd make you an offer you couldn't refuse.

•

I'm hot as a firecracker and you look like a great match.

•

I'm not free, but I am cheap! How about you?

•

Will I be driving you home in your car or mine?

•

That's a nice dress. Can you wear it to work tomorrow?

•

I would love to be the shirt on your back.

•

Is your dad a baker ... because he sure turned out a nice set of buns.

•

I'm dying to see if you're as good as you look.

•

It's cold out there. Let's go to your place and warm up under the covers.

•

Let me fly you to the moon without leaving the ground.

•

Our children to be have been wondering where you were.

•

You wanna go halves on a baby?

•

Let's get busy!

•

Read my lips: protection is perfection.

•

I'm a morning person, so why don't you spend the night?

•

This evening is rising to new heights.

•

Did I cause your martini glass to sweat?

Would you like me to call you for breakfast, or just nudge you?

•

You remind me of my fourth lover— I've only had three.

•

Can I be your Adam?

•

Would you like to fly on my magic carpet?

•

If you're beauty looking for a beast, I'm it.

•

If I were a tent, would you put me up for the night?